Diana Thompson
and Shirley Winfield

Dr Knickerbocker
Ways with Untuned Instruments
for 5–11 Year Olds

SCHOTT

Mainz · London · Madrid · New York · Paris · Tokyo · Toronto

To Desmond

Cover illustration by Joanna Bowers
Photographs by Ken Prosser and Keith Hawkins
With thanks to Darell Primary School, Richmond, Surrey
and Richard Cloudesley School, London
for permission to photograph.

CONTENTS

Dr. Knickerbocker!

Purpose:
1. To insert body percussion patterns at specified points.
2. To explore more unusual body percussion.

Keep this fast and lively
- no break between verses!

NOW! How about some surprises?

At first, the leader will be the teacher . . . Keep everyone on their toes by changing the actions.

When children are leaders they will probably want to invent their own actions — teeth gnash, eyebrow wiggle, shoulders shrug, and so on. This can be encouraged through a game of "banning" certain more obvious

You will need: Nothing - but preferably some space so that the children can stand.

actions such as clapping, stamping etc. Conversely, a nervous child could be prompted to begin with a well-known action, to gain confidence.

Tip for leaders: Only come in with your solo line — then you will have time to plan your next action, and **keep the rhythm going!** (No pauses for thought!)

First: Learn the rhyme with the following actions . . .

> *Dr. Knickerbocker, Knickerbocker, Number Nine,*
> *Sure got drunk on a bottle of wine.*
> *Let's get the rhythm of the* **(1)** *hands* (clap, clap)
> *Now we've got the rhythm of the hands* (clap, clap)

Repeat verse, with . . .   **(2)** *feet* (stamp, stamp)

(3) *eyes* (blink, blink)

(4) *knees* (knock, knock)

Always make this the last verse, so that everyone is prepared for the ending . . . →   **(5)** *hips "ooh ooh"* (slap each hip).

(End with) *Dr. Knickerbocker, Knickerbocker, Number Nine!*

"NINE" snap fingers and freeze in a comical position

Exploring words . . .

1 Words may be used: To identify and sort the natural rhythms of speech, using words and phrases (see *Orange Squash*, page 19).

Think of as many words as possible, centred around one topic (e.g. clothes) and sort them into 'sets' according to the most natural way of saying each word:

Have a quiz to see if the children can recognize the patterns you clap.

One idea is to give each child a card, with one item of clothing written on it. The teacher taps each pattern several times, changing fairly frequently from one pattern to the other. When the children match the rhythm they hear to the word on their card they stand up. They sit down when the rhythm changes.

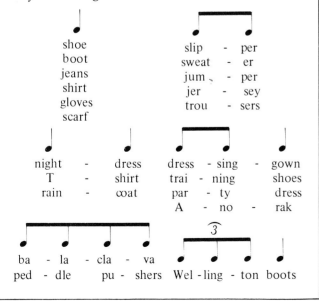

shoe	slip - per
boot	sweat - er
jeans	jum - per
shirt	jer - sey
gloves	trou - sers
scarf	

night - dress	dress - sing - gown
T - shirt	trai - ning shoes
rain - coat	par - ty dress
	A - no - rak

ba - la - cla - va
ped - dle pu - shers   Wel -ling - ton boots

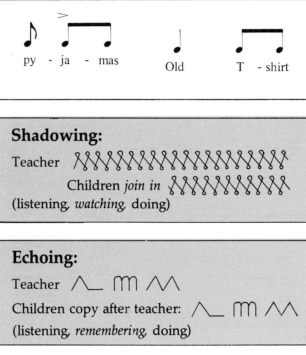

py - ja - mas   Old   T - shirt

Shadowing:

Teacher

Children *join in*

(listening, *watching*, doing)

Echoing:

Teacher

Children copy after teacher:

(listening, *remembering*, doing)

---

3 Words may be used: To use words as a reminder of tricky rhythms.

A child might invent a rhythmic ostinato (repeated pattern) and then have difficulty in remembering it when accompanying a rhyme or song. If so, it often helps to fit some words to the rhythm, which the child repeats in his head whilst playing the pattern.

4/4 Put on your py - ja - mas, and   go to bed.

---

2 Words may be used: To reinforce speech–rhythms through body percussion.

1. Take a word pattern, such as *"Wellington boot"*

- Clap the rhythm . . . or tap knees . . . or knock knuckles on the floor . . .
- Start by letting the children **shadow** your movements until the pattern is established.
- Then give them opportunity to discover other body sounds which can make the rhythm!

2. **Echo** games, e.g.:
- The teacher *says* a word pattern, then the children *clap* the rhythm; the teacher *says* another word, then the children *clap* that rhythm.

E.g. Teacher: Wellington boot   "T–shirt"

Children clap:

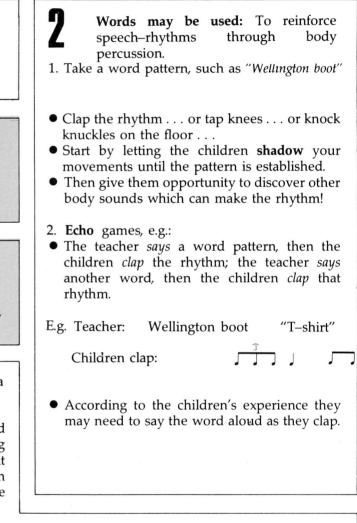

- According to the children's experience they may need to say the word aloud as they clap.

More words . . .

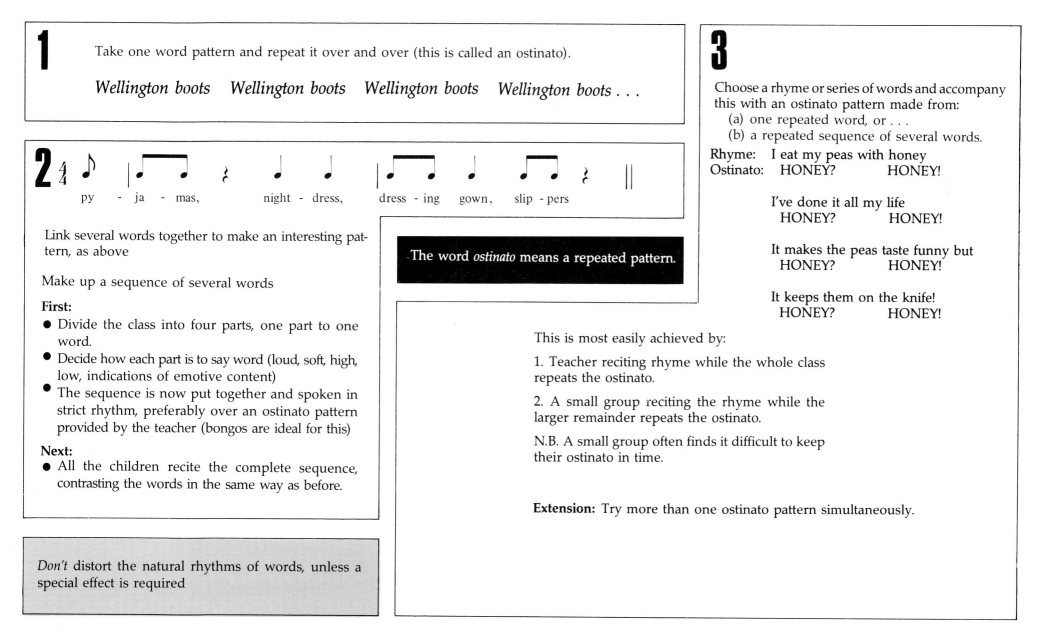

1 Take one word pattern and repeat it over and over (this is called an ostinato).

Wellington boots   Wellington boots   Wellington boots   Wellington boots . . .

2

py - ja - mas,   night - dress,   dress - ing   gown,   slip - pers

Link several words together to make an interesting pattern, as above

Make up a sequence of several words

First:
- Divide the class into four parts, one part to one word.
- Decide how each part is to say word (loud, soft, high, low, indications of emotive content)
- The sequence is now put together and spoken in strict rhythm, preferably over an ostinato pattern provided by the teacher (bongos are ideal for this)

Next:
- All the children recite the complete sequence, contrasting the words in the same way as before.

Don't distort the natural rhythms of words, unless a special effect is required

The word *ostinato* means a repeated pattern.

3

Choose a rhyme or series of words and accompany this with an ostinato pattern made from:
  (a) one repeated word, or . . .
  (b) a repeated sequence of several words.

Rhyme: I eat my peas with honey
Ostinato: HONEY?   HONEY!

I've done it all my life
  HONEY?   HONEY!

It makes the peas taste funny but
  HONEY?   HONEY!

It keeps them on the knife!
  HONEY?   HONEY!

This is most easily achieved by:

1. Teacher reciting rhyme while the whole class repeats the ostinato.

2. A small group reciting the rhyme while the larger remainder repeats the ostinato.

N.B. A small group often finds it difficult to keep their ostinato in time.

Extension: Try more than one ostinato pattern simultaneously.

Still more words . . .

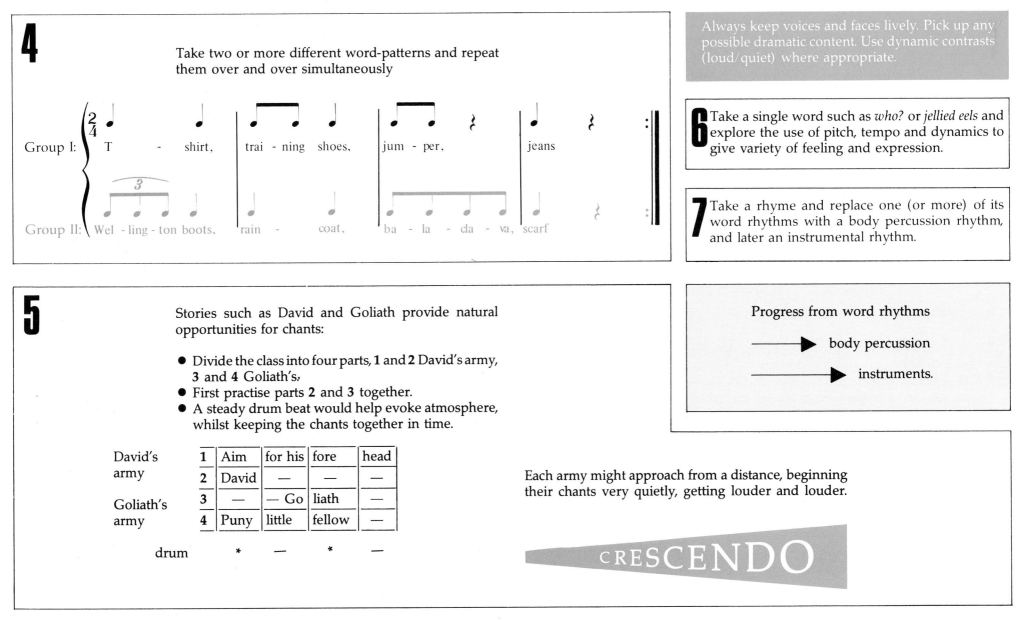

4 Take two or more different word-patterns and repeat them over and over simultaneously

Group I: T-shirt, trai-ning shoes, jum-per, jeans

Group II: Wel-ling-ton boots, rain-coat, ba-la-cla-va, scarf

6 Take a single word such as *who?* or *jellied eels* and explore the use of pitch, tempo and dynamics to give variety of feeling and expression.

7 Take a rhyme and replace one (or more) of its word rhythms with a body percussion rhythm, and later an instrumental rhythm.

5 Stories such as David and Goliath provide natural opportunities for chants:

- Divide the class into four parts, **1** and **2** David's army, **3** and **4** Goliath's.
- First practise parts **2** and **3** together.
- A steady drum beat would help evoke atmosphere, whilst keeping the chants together in time.

Progress from word rhythms

⟶ body percussion

⟶ instruments.

David's army	**1** Aim	for his	fore	head
	2 David	—	—	—
Goliath's army	**3** —	— Go	liath	—
	4 Puny	little	fellow	—
drum	*	—	*	—

Each army might approach from a distance, beginning their chants very quietly, getting louder and louder.

CRESCENDO

Number tossing

You will need: space for a circle.

Purpose: Group awareness of pulse

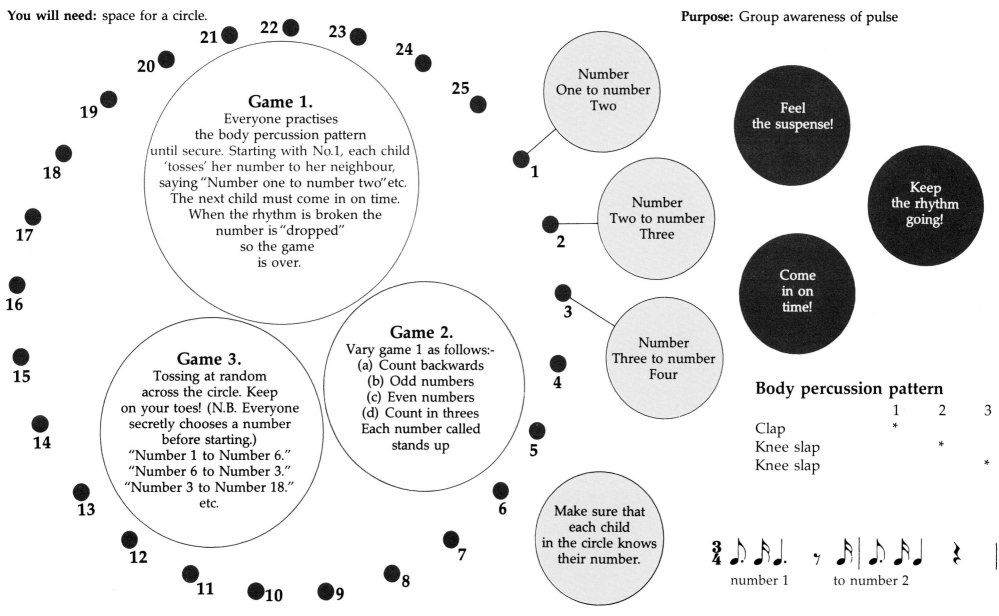

Game 1.
Everyone practises
the body percussion pattern
until secure. Starting with No.1, each child
'tosses' her number to her neighbour,
saying "Number one to number two" etc.
The next child must come in on time.
When the rhythm is broken the
number is "dropped"
so the game
is over.

Game 3.
Tossing at random
across the circle. Keep
on your toes! (N.B. Everyone
secretly chooses a number
before starting.)
"Number 1 to Number 6."
"Number 6 to Number 3."
"Number 3 to Number 18."
etc.

Game 2.
Vary game 1 as follows:-
(a) Count backwards
(b) Odd numbers
(c) Even numbers
(d) Count in threes
Each number called
stands up

Number
One to number
Two

Number
Two to number
Three

Number
Three to number
Four

Make sure that
each child
in the circle knows
their number.

Feel
the suspense!

Keep
the rhythm
going!

Come
in on
time!

Body percussion pattern

	1	2	3
Clap	*		
Knee slap		*	
Knee slap			*

number 1   to number 2

Left right left!

You will need:
1. Large space - a hall
2. either: right shoes off, left shoes on!
   or: tie bell ribbons around left ankles

Listen to those Left Feet!

Left . . . left,
Left, right, left!
Left . . . left,
Left, right, left!
If . . . wrong, you must
Change your step
Left . . . left,
Left, right, left!

Purpose:
1. Developing sense of pulse
2. Awareness of left and right

At first everyone 'marks time' until the left feet all sound together. Practise doing this with the chant.

Leader weaves path through hall. All chant words as they march in time . . .

Try marching to music:
- Teacher plays a drum rhythm or . . .
- group of children play repeated patterns on instruments or . . .
- play a record of bright music in march time

Diddle diddle dumpling (a cumulative game)

You will need: Standing room.

Before playing this game the children should have had many opportunities to explore the wide variety of body percussion sounds possible, e.g. finger snap, clap, knee, slap, stamp, cheek pop, knuckle rub, chest thump etc.

● Now we can begin . . . This is a cumulative game which each time it is played should be built up stage by stage as follows:-

Purpose:
1. To encourage imaginative use of a wide variety of body percussion.
2. To present a means of memorising a body percussion sequence through the use of words.
3. To develop internal listening.

Diddle, diddle dumpling, my son John
Went to bed with his trousers on,
One shoe off and one shoe on,
Diddle, diddle dumpling, my son John.

● Ask the children to *interpret* this rhyme in as many varied ways as possible:
e.g. angrily — loudly
shocked — whispered
reprimanding John — children waggling their fingers at each other.

Encourage lively facial expressions and voice inflections.

Start together! One child claps or stamps a pattern such as "My son John", twice before everyone enters. This might make an effective accompaniment throughout.

NB: Suggested movements which make no sound, e.g. shoulder tap, are valid as they provide an active experience of a silent beat.

Extension: Substitute instruments for body percussion.

---

1. Recite rhyme.	Always speak energetically, standing up.
2. Recite rhyme substituting ★ ★ for 'trousers'.	★ ★ For this first substitution always make two finger snaps simultaneously with two tongue clicks to match the two syllables in the word 'trousers'. Practise it in strict time like this:- (say) trous-ers ★ ★ trousers ★ ★ click click click click.
3. Repeat rhyme substituting ★ ★ for 'trousers' and ☐ for 'shoe' (twice)	☐ For this substitution ask the children for ideas and likewise to the end of the game.
4. Repeat rhyme substituting ★ ★ for 'trousers', ☐ for 'shoe' and ☆ ☆ ☆ for 'my son John'	For these, encourage varying combinations e.g. ☆ ☆ ☆ knees clap cheek pop
5. Repeat rhyme substituting ★ ★ for 'trousers' ☐ for 'shoe' ☆ ☆ ☆ for 'my son John' and ✪✪ ✪✪ ✪ ✪ for Diddle, diddle dumpling.	

EXPLORING SOUND . . .

Make a collection of sound-makers, using the following categories as a guide:
- wooden objects
- metal objects
- hollow objects
- surfaces that can be scraped
- objects that can be suspended

The children will soon discover other categories. **One** category at a time on the music table will encourage more imaginative experimentation.

Ask:
- Which produces the highest sound?
- Which produces the lowest sound?
- Can you find five objects of different pitches?
- Can you place them in a high to low, or low to high order?
- Which produces the longest sound?
- Which produces the shortest sound?

Purpose: to discover that different materials produce different timbres. To explore pitch, dynamics, duration, and other concepts.

Remember: there is not necessarily a right answer to these questions, because most natural sound-makers produce overtones which are heard differently by different people.

Put one interesting object, such as a tea pot, watering-can or biscuit tin on to a table. Make a collection of beaters and brushes - metal rods, chopsticks, toothbrushes, plastic spoons and large screws are a few of the possibilities. Remember to put out conventional beaters, too.

Ask:
- Does the teapot always make the same sound when it is tapped (or brushed)?
- How many sounds can you help it to make?
- Which beaters make good quiet sounds?
- Which beaters make good loud sounds?
- What happens to the sound when you bounce the striker?
- What happens when you do not bounce the striker?

Purpose: To discover that the sound potential of any object is dependant upon the type of striker used; thus a wide variety of sound is possible.

Implication In any music playing, the *kind* of beater/hammer/striker/brush/bow used, and *the way it is played* is of fundamental importance to the quality of the sound produced.

Collect many containers of different size, shape and material.

Put six dried peas (or any other suitable substance that can be exactly measured) inside each container.

The containers can now be shaken:

Ask:
- Do the peas sound the same in each container?
- Which make the loudest sound?
- Which make the quietest sound?
- is one higher/lower than the others?
- Can you guess which container the peas are in now? (A screen or large box is useful here).

Purpose To discover that different kinds of resonating surfaces will produce different kinds of sounds.

Implications: Care is needed to avoid cracks and scratches on the surfaces of instruments, as this will adversely affect the sound.

Choice of the container is an important element when making shakers.

Collect several identical containers. Transparent ones are useful for very young children. Each should have different contents (rice, lentils, sand, dried peas, beads, etc.).
The containers should now be shaken.

Ask:
- Do the containers all look the same?
- Do they all sound the same?
- Which makes a rattling sound?
- Which makes a shuffling sound?
- Can you think of words to describe the sound of each container?

Purpose: To discover that varying contents will produce different sounds.

Implications: When making their own shakers, the children need freedom to experiment with varying contents until they find the sound that satisfies them. Thus this activity involves not only artistic judgements and dexterity, but the making of musical choices and decisions.

Place several contrasting objects on the music table. Collect many kinds of beaters, factory-made and unconventional, e.g.:

soft rubber	wooden
hard rubber	metal
felt	chopstick
wool	spoon

Ask:
- Strike each object with the felt beater - does it produce a good sound from each object?
- Take each object in turn, and find the beater which produces a sound that satisfies you.
- Does each object sound good with the same beater?
- Which kind of material needs hard beaters?
- Which kind needs softer beaters?
- Does it matter **where** you strike each object with the beater?
- Did you find any unexpected sounds?

Purpose: To develop judgement in the choice of beater that will produce the required sound.

Implication: When seeking a specific timbre, children will be more discriminating in the choice and use of beater.

Selection and experimentation are valid musical activities which do not necessarily require an end result such as performance.

In order to concentrate on specific concepts, while experimenting with these sound-makers, quizzes can be devised. A screen or large box, in which to hide the objects, adds to the fun.

These experimental sound-makers can be used most effectively in a musical piece when required. One easily organised activity is to choose an evocative poem, and ask the children to make decisions as to appropriate "instrumentation". The atmosphere produced by environmental sound-sources can be surprisingly effective. (See page 14)

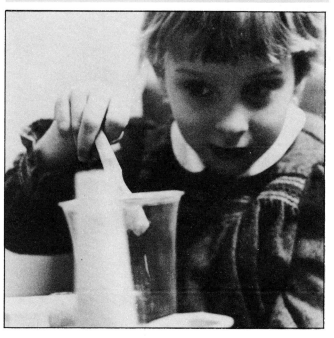

EXPLORING WITH HANDS . . .

How many sounds can you find using only your hands?

Try:
- clapping with flat hands
- clapping with cupped hands
- clapping using fingers only
- clapping two fingers on palm
- stroking palms in circular movements
- stroking using a variety of hand shapes from cupped to stretched.
- rubbing hands back to back
- tapping knuckles
- rubbing knuckles against each other (scraping effect)
- snapping fingers
- flicking fingers against palm
- rubbing fingernails against each other
- holding one hand against ear and experimenting with the other.

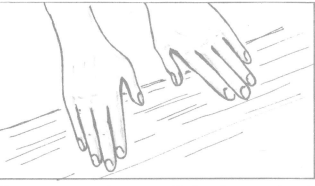

How many sounds can you find, using your hands and fingers, on table or floor?

Try:
- pattering your fingers quickly on the pads
- pattering your fingers using fingernails
- pattering with stiff, flat fingers
- pattering with whole hand
- stroking surface with palm using a circular movement
- gently stroking surface using fingernails
- knocking or rapping with knuckles
- slapping surface with flat hand
- slapping surface with cupped hand
- thumping with clenched fist
- placing one hand flat on surface, then with free hand striking flat hand and surface alternately.

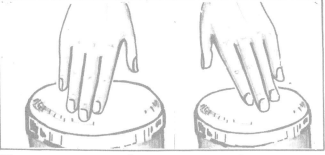

How many sounds can you make on your instruments (tuned and untuned), using hands and fingers?

Try (according to instrument - it may not always work):
- tapping with flat fingers
- tapping with pads of fingers
- tapping with fingernails
- tapping with palm
- striking with pad at base of thumb
- stroking with palm of hand (circular or straight movement as appropriate to instrument)
- scraping with back of hand using nails
- gently scratching surface with nails (drums only)
- tapping with knuckles
- flicking fingers
- tapping as shown on tambourine, for a neat rhythm with no sound of jingles.

Thumb pressed still against skin of tambourine, tap thumb with fingernail of other hand, keeping thumb firm.

for jingle trill, lick thumb and skim it around the edge of the skin causing friction.

EXPLORING WITH beads, drawing pins, screws, rice, ping pong balls

How many sounds can you make on your instruments (tuned or untuned), using items from the "make-more-sounds" tray?

Keep experimenting — the possibilities are endless.

Try:

- Bouncing a ping pong ball on a drum (controlling it with a cupped hand, close to the surface) and letting it rebound several times
- Rolling a ping pong ball around the inside perimeter of a drum, controlling its speed by a gentle rocking movement
- Stopping the above by holding the drum almost vertical and absolutely still, allowing the ball to come to rest in its own time (it will swing like a pendulum).
- Dropping rice, drawing pins, etc. into a drum; sliding from side to side, tapping from underneath — experiment!
- Scattering upturned drawing pins on to glockenspiel bars; tapping bars at random with beater (pins will vibrate).
- Drawing string of beads, chain, teazle, ridged handle of beater against vibrating edge of instrument.

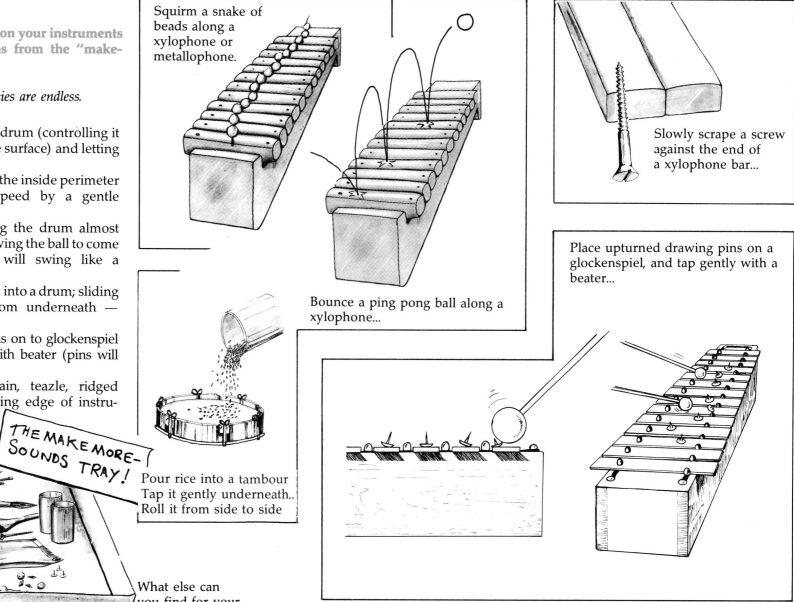

THE MAKE MORE-SOUNDS TRAY!

Squirm a snake of beads along a xylophone or metallophone.

Bounce a ping pong ball along a xylophone...

Slowly scrape a screw against the end of a xylophone bar...

Place upturned drawing pins on a glockenspiel, and tap gently with a beater...

Pour rice into a tambour Tap it gently underneath... Roll it from side to side

What else can you find for your Make-more-sounds Tray?

11

You will need:
1. Space for a seated circle
2. One untuned instrument for each child - as wide a variety as possible.

Purpose:
1. To discover the natural duration of instruments
2. To develop concentrated listening
3. To develop controlled response and quick reaction.

PLAY ONE BY ONE . . .

Ready steady one!

The children sit in a circle with the instruments and beaters in front of them. The teacher plays a long quiet sound, e.g. on triangle, which is the signal for the children to pick up their instruments *silently*. When the sound has completely died away, the first child plays her instrument, followed one by one by each child around the circle.

WAIT FOR THE PREVIOUS SOUND TO DIE AWAY BEFORE PLAYING

Questions:
Which instruments have long sounds?
Which have very short sounds?
Are the longest sounds made by wooden, metal or skin instruments?

PLAY ONE BY ONE WITHOUT LEAVING A SOUND GAP . . .

Ready steady two!

Now for the tricky part . . .

First: Choose one cymbal player and neighbour. Ask the neighbour: "Can you play your sound as soon as the cymbal has died away, but *without leaving a sound gap?*" Question after demonstration to ensure that everyone understands.
Then: Choose one woodblock player. "Who thinks they can play their sound *immediately* the woodblock dies away?"
Now for the game: Now each child plays around the circle as before, trying to ensure that they *wait . . . then play immediately!*

The contrast between the control required while waiting for a long sound to end, and the alertness necessary to play immediately after a short sound creates an exciting and absorbing activity.

and 3 . . .

You will need: As for Game One

Purpose:
1. To encourage unconventional ways of varying the duration of the instruments
2. To develop concentrated listening
3. To develop controlled response and quick reaction

Beforehand
Experiment to find ways in which the normal duration of the instruments can be reversed.

e.g.

- Strike a cymbal loudly, then damp it immediately, either against the body or between two fingers.

- Continuously shake maracas

- Rub two claves together to produce continuous sound

- Scrape fingers around drum head.

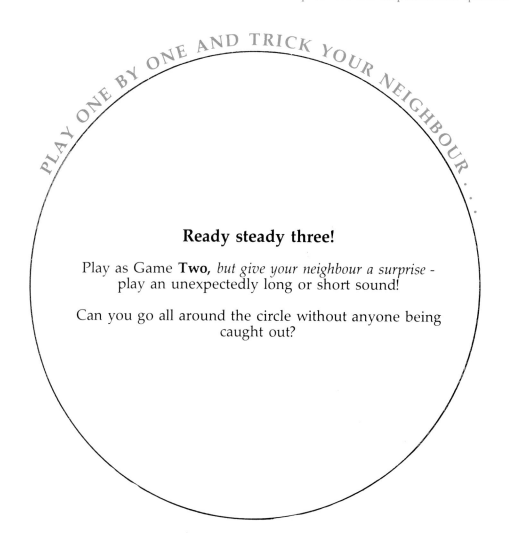

PLAY ONE BY ONE AND TRICK YOUR NEIGHBOUR . . .

Ready steady three!

Play as Game **Two,** *but give your neighbour a surprise -* play an unexpectedly long or short sound!

Can you go all around the circle without anyone being caught out?

I saw three witches

(arranged by Caroline Pentland)

You will need:
1. Previous experience of making imaginative sounds with voices, hands and instruments.
2. A selection of instruments.

This verse could be set in many different ways.
Ask the children for suggestions. Always *try out* their ideas before deciding whether or not they are suitable.

If your children have had very little experience in setting a verse, try the following arrangement. However, do be flexible - if another idea is suggested, incorporate it, if possible. In this arrangement the verse is repeated *three times* as follows:

1 One child, a group, or the whole class, recite the verse (remember . . . *expressive voices and faces!)*

Purpose: To make a setting of a poem, using a variety of imaginative sounds (see pages 8/9), in particular various kinds of tremolos (see pages 10/11) produced by voices, hands, and instruments.

> *I saw three witches*
> *That sailed in a shallop*
> *All turning their heads with a smickering smile,*
> *Till a bank of green osiers**
> *Concealed their grim faces*
> *Though I heard them lamenting for many a mile*
>
> (from "I saw three witches" by Walter de la Mare)
>
> * willows

2 **You will need:**
3 solo voices (Voice 1 Voice 2 Voice 3)
A witches group (for witches' cackles)
Large group (the remainder)

I saw three witches . . . (*Three solo voices,* one after the other, speaking the words **meaningfully!**)

    I saw three witches . . .

        I saw three witches . . . (Spoken **witchily,** in turn)

            They sailed in a shallop . . . (followed by **Cackles** from Witches' group)

                That sailed in a shallop . . .

                    That sailed in a shallop

Large Group: All turrrning their heads with a sssmickering smile . . .

                Till a bank of green osiers concealed their grim faces . . .

                    Till a bank of green osiers concealed their grim faces . . .

                      Till a bank of green osiers concealed their grim faces . . . *Witches' group:* **eerie cackles . . .**

Large group: Though I heard them **lamenting** for many a mile.

                All: make lamenting sounds with voices (e.g. descending ahhhhhh ahhhhhh sounds)

3

You will need:

1. Instruments (tuned or untuned) to make water and osier sounds. (One or two tuned instruments might play a witchlike repeated pattern throughout)
2. The remainder divided into(1) witches (2) water (3) osiers

---

Vocal tremolos

A group cackling - experience with gleeful cackling, menacing cackling, quiet eerie cackling . . .
A group lamenting - try to make their lamenting sounds mysterious, and maybe rather sinister.

Group 2:	I saw three witches
Witches:	**Cackles**
Group 3:	That sailed in a shallop
Groups 2 and 3:	**Shallop music with voices and hands**
All:	All turning their heads with a smickering smile
Group 2:	Till a bank of green osiers
Groups 2 and 3:	**Osier sounds with instruments and hands**
Group 3:	Concealed their grim faces
Witches:	**Cackles**
Groups 2 and 3:	Though I heard them lamenting for many a mile
All:	**Lamenting sounds, instruments, etc., slowly fade out, leaving an eerie stillness.**

Group 1 cackles and screeches appropriately
Groups 2 and 3 make sounds with their mouths, lips (fast finger-wobble over lips) and voices: sshsshing, slurping, hissing, slapping, etc.

More tremolos

Voices: as before, with the addition of water sounds (see "you need . . .")
Hands: try to get different sounds for "shallop" and "osier" music. Brush flat hands, squeeze cupped hands, drum fingers, etc. (see p.10)

Instruments: be as imaginative as possible, in order to evoke the atmosphere needed.

Could you find place for: knuckle-rub? (scrape knuckles across each other for a grinding sound)

15

Car wash

You will need:
1. Preferably to have visited a nearby car wash, if several children have not experienced it.
2. Instruments for half the class.
3. Space for movement for half the class.

1 Discuss the characteristics of a car wash machine.(If possible visit one. Take a stop watch and time each action, starting with the coin dropping. A parent might take some of the children inside their car . . . Much language work, and mathematics will result.)
The main characteristics which emerge will possibly be:
- The coin drops . . . immediate activity.
- The swirling brushes, working in particular sequence, on all four sides of the car.
- The machinery supporting the brushes, squirting water, air, etc., working in a particular sequence.
- The comparative size of the car wash and the car itself.
- The sudden ending . . . brushes becoming still . . . complete stillness and quietness . . . car moves on.
- The complete sequence begins all over again with the next car.

2 First form small groups
- Explore the variety of sounds, making imaginative use of instruments and more unconventional sound makers.
- Explore the movement aspects.

What other machinery would provide a starting point for similar work? . . .

Purpose
1. To give experience of inventing repeated patterns and textures which evoke the efficiency of this machine.
2. To work alongside a movement group.

3 It will be found that larger groups are necessary. The car wash will need many children making roly-poly arm movements upwards and downwards, synchronising their movements carefully, besides the other parts of the machine, and the car itself. Half the class moving and half playing should be ideal.

Combine harvester

You will need:
1. Instruments for half the class
2. Space for movement, preferably the hall.

This work would need several sessions. If possible, *all* the class should experience the movement, and *all* should have taken part in the instrumental work.

Might this form part of your harvest festival?

Purpose:
1. To give experience of inventing patterns and textures which evoke the power of this machine.

2. To experience ‹crescendo and diminuendo›

3. To work alongside a movement group.

1 Discuss the characteristics of a combine harvester. A comparison with previous methods (e.g. men with scythes) might by contrast indicate the power, noise, and efficiency of this machine.

2 All form groups. Try to show, by movement, the parts of the machine which rotate, which move in a different way, and so on. Remember the driver. What movements does he make? What path would a combine harvester take, and why?

3 It will be found that larger groups are necessary. Some children may continue working on the movement aspects whilst others now form small groups with untuned instruments.

4 The instrumental groups build up repeated patterns (see page 29). Whilst working in groups it is helpful if they work quietly. However, the instruments chosen must have the potential to make large strong sounds. Hard sounds, and metal sounds will evoke the quality of machinery.

5 Hear the groups separately, ask them to begin very quietly, get louder and louder, then gradually quieter. This will describe the machine getting nearer and nearer, passing by, and going away.

6 Try all the groups together. First give a pulse, and ensure that each group can play in time with it. (This combination of groups may, or may not sound effective but give it a try.) Otherwise select one group's piece, and help the remaining instrumentalists to contribute to it.

7 When both music and movement groups have been worked out, try them together. The harvester might wait outside the door... the music quietly begins... the harvester enters and moves around the hall towards the music group (*crescendo*) passes by, and moves out towards and through the door (*diminuendo*).

Treasure hunt! Sounds guide the treasure-seeker

You will need
1. Chalk or masking tape to mark out a course along the hall floor
2. A large selection of conventional and unconventional sound-makers
3. A blindfold

Before the game
Divide the class into five groups, using contrasting sound-makers, as indicated in the diagram
Each group invents a short sequence which can be repeated indefinitely, except for the **stop** group, whose sequence is played only once.

The game

Each group is now ready to use its music as a signal to guide the Treasure Seeker along the course from *Start* to *Finish*
(e.g. *metal* sounds signal *move forward*; *skins* signal *stop*, *etc.* at the appropriate time)
Choose one child to be Treasure Seeker, and blindfold her. . .
Now her only option is to listen . . . and interpret the sound signals correctly!
All the instrumentalists watch her progress carefully — they must start only when the preceding *stop* signal has sounded and been observed.
The appropriate group continues to repeat its sequence until the next *stop* signal is played. Ensure that the stop signal group is alert, as it is particularly responsible for the Treasure Seeker's accuracy.

As long as the five groups have a distinctive sound any form of contrast can be used, e.g. duration. . . dynamics . . . tempo . . . pitch . . . etc.

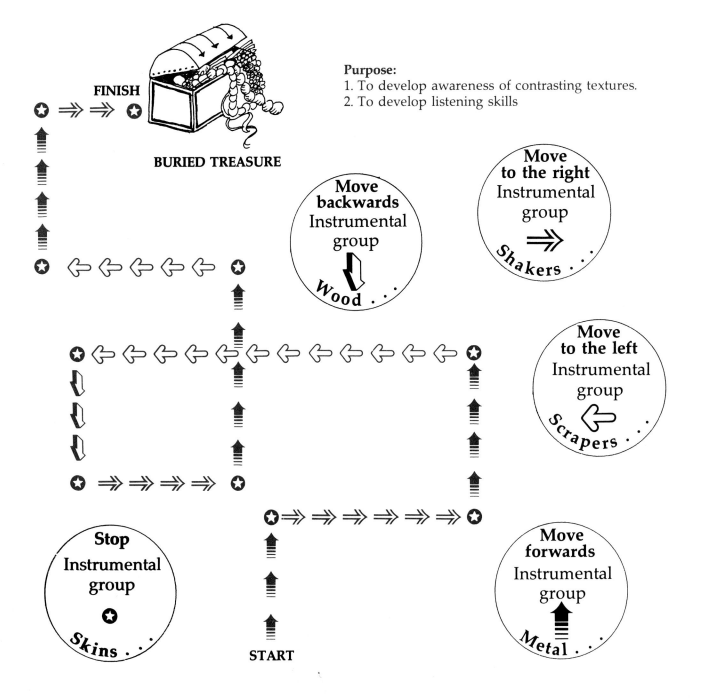

Purpose:
1. To develop awareness of contrasting textures.
2. To develop listening skills

Orange squash

You will need: 1 orange, 5-6 hand percussion instruments, e.g. 1 each of the following:- Woodblock tambour, Indian bells, maracas, triangle, guiro, one pair of cymbals. One child holds cymbals throughout game, remaining in the centre with the instruments. She plays at "SQUASH".

Purpose: To identify and sort word rhythms

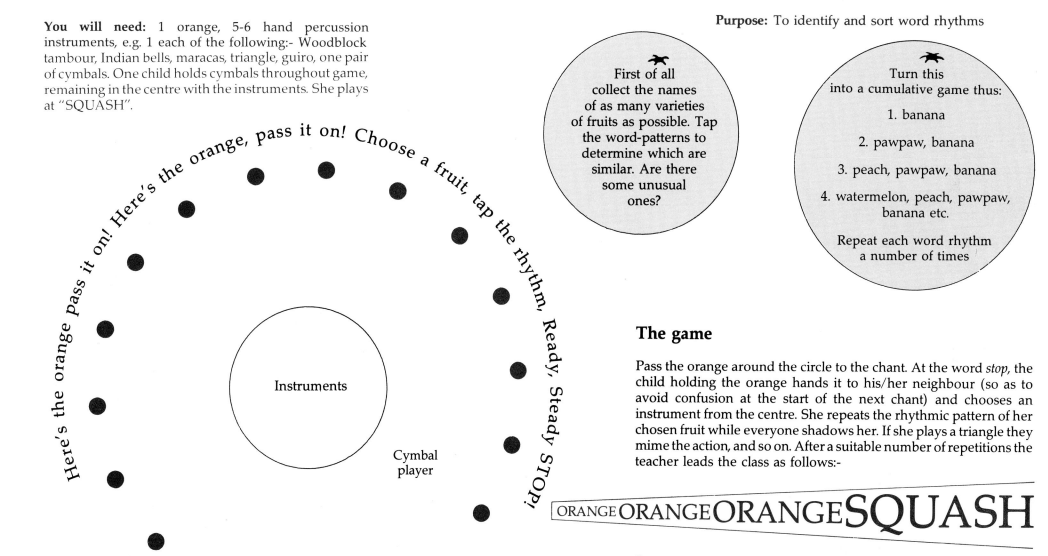

Here's the orange Pass it on! Here's the orange, pass it on! Choose a fruit, tap the rhythm, Ready, Steady STOP!

Instruments

Cymbal player

First of all collect the names of as many varieties of fruits as possible. Tap the word-patterns to determine which are similar. Are there some unusual ones?

Turn this into a cumulative game thus:

1. banana

2. pawpaw, banana

3. peach, pawpaw, banana

4. watermelon, peach, pawpaw, banana etc.

Repeat each word rhythm a number of times

The game

Pass the orange around the circle to the chant. At the word *stop*, the child holding the orange hands it to his/her neighbour (so as to avoid confusion at the start of the next chant) and chooses an instrument from the centre. She repeats the rhythmic pattern of her chosen fruit while everyone shadows her. If she plays a triangle they mime the action, and so on. After a suitable number of repetitions the teacher leads the class as follows:-

ORANGE ORANGE ORANGE SQUASH

Open arms gradually to match the crescendo . . . loud clap on "SQUASH". The child with the instrument takes it back to her place and continues to play her pattern while the rest continue with the chant. The game ends when all the instruments have been used.

19

Untuned instruments - The closer to the body, the easier to play

Understanding what is involved technically helps to sort out problems when they occur
(The arrows suggest the development towards the next stage)

EARLY STAGES

1 ➡	**2** ➡	**3** ➡
Sound produced <u>automatically</u> by natural body movements, while instruments are worn or held.	Sound produced <u>intentionally</u> by both hands equally.	Sound produced by striking or brushing with one hand.
Instrument felt as an extension of the body.	Instrument felt as an extension of the body.	One hand holds the instrument while the other strikes or brushes in direct contact with the vibrating surface.
Direct contact with instrument.	Both hands in direct contact and equally balanced.	Contact unequal - one hand holds while the other strikes.

Maracas, Sleigh Bell Spray, Sleigh Bell anklet, Bell Spray.

Pair of Cymbals, Maracas, Indian Bells, Claves.

Tambourine (those without screws are the lightest and easiest to play), Bell Spray, Sleigh Bell Spray, Shaker, Tambour, Jingles rattle, (not shown, see p24).

The sleigh bells spray and bell spray may be tapped with the other hand to produce a crisp rhythm.

20

Holding one or two beaters requires more dexterity.

4 \\\\\\⮕

5

Sound produced by striking or scraping with one beater.	Sound produced by striking with two beaters
One hand holds the instrument while the other holds a beater. Thus the point of contact is several centimeters away from the hand.	Both hands hold beaters. There is now no direct contact with the instrument.
Contact unequal, - one hand holds while the other strikes.	Neither hand in contact, but the balance now equal.

Checklist for ordering instruments
(to help ensure a good balance of texture).

Preparation for two beaters.

Hands on knees ⮕

⮕ Hands on table ⮕

⮕ Beaters on table ⮕

⮕ Beaters on instruments

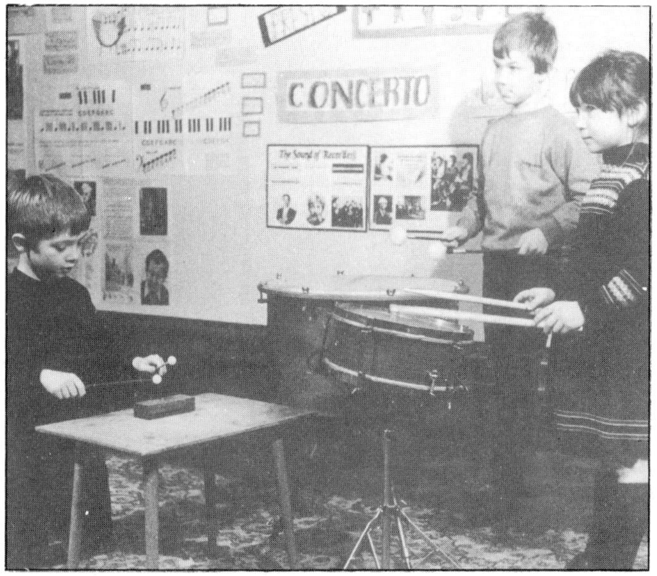

Metal		Skin
Indian Bells (finger cymbals)		Tambour
Triangle		Tambourine
Cymbals:	– one with beater	Bongos
	– one on stand	Conga
Gong	– pair	Bass Drum
Sleigh bells		Side Drum
Jingles rattle		Timpani
Tambourine		
Bell Tree		
Multi-guiro		
Cowbells		
Agogo bells (Latin American)		

Wood

Claves (rhythm sticks)
Woodblock
Two-tone block (tubular)
Tulip Woodblock
Temple Blocks (set of three to five on a stand)
Wooden Agogo
Castanets
Guiro (Resi resi)
Gato Drum
Barrel Drum
Side Drum
Timpani

Hollow shell or gourd

Maracas
Cabasa
Shakers
Guiro

Bell tree, Fish guiro, Single cymbal and beater, Triangle, Woodblock, Tambour and wire brush.

Woodblock with two beaters, Timpani, Side drum.

Ways with drums . . .

Care for your instruments!

- Put vaseline around the screws of drums to prevent them from going stiff.
- Loosen the screws when not in use to prevent the frames from buckling.
- Keep instruments away from heaters to prevent warping, drying and cracking.
- Remember that a cracked instrument produces poor sound.
- Children may enjoy making decorative cloth bags which can be hung up for easy storage as well as giving the instruments protection.

Ethnic instruments

Search around in ethnic craft shops for unusual and often inexpensive instruments.
Cowbells, Rattles, Wind Chimes, Indian Bells . . .

Toy shops

Look for:
Pop guns, Bird whistles, Sirens, Metal clickers, Football Rattles, Swannee whistles, Kazoos . . .

Skin instruments (drums and tambourines)

Normal tambour hold

Between knees, played with both hands

Between knees, pressing skin to alter pitch

Flat on knees, played with both hands

Tips on Technique

Upturned tambourine, both hands tap rim

Tremolos (or rolls)

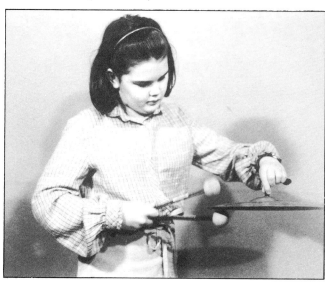

Cymbal roll: Separate two beaters with forefinger and grip firmly in one hand. Slide cymbal in between heads of beaters and trill rapidly.

Tambourine trill: for a really effective trill dampen thumb (slightly) and skid it along the rim. This vibrates the skin which then vibrates the jingles.

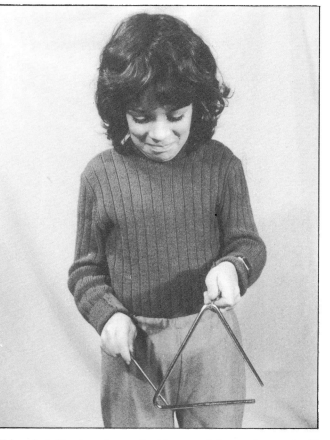

Triangle trill: place beater inside one of the angles, and trill rapidly across the corner.

More tips on Technique . . .

General techniques

Jingles rattle, tapped with jingles horizontal.

Cabasa: either rest on the palm of one hand, and twist the handle backwards and forwards with the other, or hold handle with one hand, and tap beads with the other.

One clave is placed across cupped hand forming a 'sound box'. Strike with the other clave. The hollow shape will give greater resonance.

Sleigh bell spray tapped against hip.

Indian bells (finger cymbals): a pair fixed in each hand can be used effectively in movement and dance. Playing these requires dexterity, but the challenge is exciting.

Cymbal tapped with metal striker.

Meet some multitones...

In this book there is frequent reference to "multitones". These can be provided by some conventional instruments (such as those on this page) **which produce two or more different sounds** but are played by one player.

Agogo bells

"Percussion Tree"

Bongos on stand

Two-tone block (Tubular wood block)

Wooden Agogo (scrape or strike)

Set of two timpani (rotational tuning)

Medium-sized Gato Drum

...make a multi-tone

Two or three tambours or tambourines placed on the floor, preferably on a carpet or soft cloth, give an effect similar to timpani when played with two beaters

Select three to five instruments such as cowbells, agogo bells, woodblocks, triangle or cymbals. Clamp or string them on to a secure stand such as a clothes horse or dowelling across a music stand. Provide a variety of beaters. Try a hard beater in one hand and a soft one in the other.

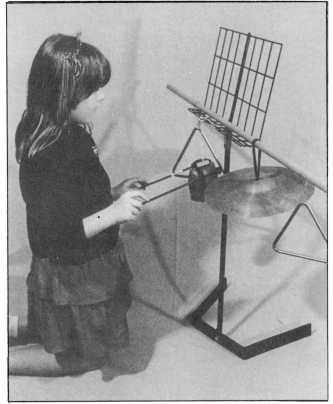

Metal instruments hung from dowelling.

Take two or three different sized cymbals or triangles, string them from a metal coat hanger or music stand and play them with two beaters.

Here an assortment of metal objects has been suspended from a gong stand.

ONE PERSON . . .   SEVERAL SOUNDS . . .   MAKES A MULTITONE!

Do-it-yourself multitones

Kitchenalia!

Collect two to five kitchen objects that can be tapped, e.g. set of graded, plastic containers, enamel items, wooden spoons, saucepan lids, **or** find some scraping sounds, e.g. cheese grater, egg slicer.

Could you make a *Garden shed* multitone?

Collect items which can be suspended from a coat rack stand, e.g. clay flower pots, shelf brackets, copper tubing, even horseshoes, and strike with two selected beaters.

Try fastening three to five bicycle bells of different pitches to a firm base. Experiment to find suitable strikers. A clock chime, and the inside of a toy piano have been added here.

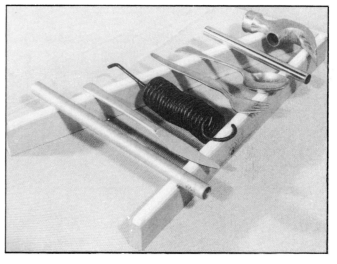

Surprise strips

Take two strips of wood, each roughly the length and width of a ruler and about one centimeter thick. Stick a strip of one centimeter wide foamdraught excluder along the narrow edge. Place the strips of wood, foam side uppermost, alongside each other about eight centimeters apart. (Adjust this space as necessary).

Now
1. Place ANY metal objects across the strips of wood, and strike with two metal beaters. Try forks, spoons, screws, nails, skewers, copper tubing, and the most surprising sounds will emerge!

Or...
2. Place any wooden or bamboo items across the strips - claves or woodblocks can be included. Select five to eight varying pitches. They should sound bright when struck by wooden beaters. This combination can produce the most appealing multitone.

27

EXPLORING MUSICAL IDEAS . . .

Eenie, Meenie, Gypsa Leenie

You will need: space - a hall or playground

Purpose: To experience pulse through body movement.

Chant rhythmically:

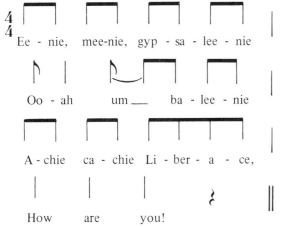

Ee - nie, mee-nie, gyp - sa - lee - nie

Oo - ah um __ ba - lee - nie

A - chie ca - chie Li - ber - a - ce,

How are you!

This American playground game is traditionally played in a circle, with the three clap pattern described below. Each repetition is faster than the previous one. In the original game, children must drop out if they miss a clap. The last one left is the winner.

L.H. claps upwards on beats 1 & 2; whilst R.H. claps downwards on beats 1 & 2; Clap own hands together on beat 3

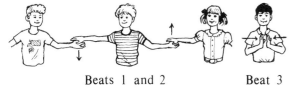

Beats 1 and 2   Beat 3

This three beat clapping pattern produces a counter rhythm to the four beat chant. This is a characteristic of many playground games. Children find this quite easy, and it adds to the fun.

Fill the gap

You will need: Sufficient instruments for half the class. Space for two circles seated one inside the other.

1 Give each child in the inner circle an instrument which they place on the floor.

2 Both circles do as follows:-

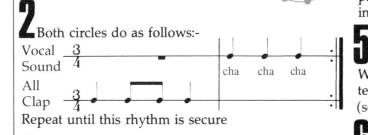

Repeat until this rhythm is secure

3 Same as above but this time leave the second bar (cha cha cha) *silent*, thinking these three beats internally. This produces a *sound gap!* There is a natural tendency for the tempo to increase. Guard against this.

Purpose: To enable children to invent short patterns on instruments, with the help of preliminary echo work.

4 Now it is time to fill the gap. The inside circle picks up their instruments. The outside circle continues its clapping pattern, and one by one around the circle the players produce the three crotchet beats on their instruments.

5 *Vary the filling . . .* (essential preparation for no.6) While the outer circle continues to clap as before, the teacher gives patterns for all the players to imitate:- (see example)

6 Now play *Fill the Gap* one by one around the circle (as in No.4). Encourage the players to vary both the rhythms and the dynamics.

7 Change the circles around so that the "clappers" become the players.

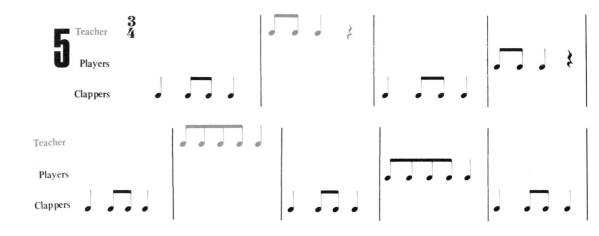

Ostinato building

You will need: A selection of untuned instruments.

Ostinato building is like building a wall . . .

First lay the foundations (the pulse):

Then the first row of bricks (one instrument):

Then the second row (another instrument)

Then the next . . .

(And the next . . .

And the next . . .)

Use ostinato building
- to form accompaniments to rhymes and songs. (see page 32)
- to play an accompaniment for a musical game (see page 33)
- to play an accompaniment whilst other instruments are *improvising.*

Purpose:

1. To encourage awareness of other parts (There is no conductor, so players must *listen* to keep in time).

2. To provide a means of inventing accompaniments on the spot.

3. To help groups working in playtimes by providing a means of building up a piece effectively and quickly. A complete piece, including improvisations, can be built up within the short time available.

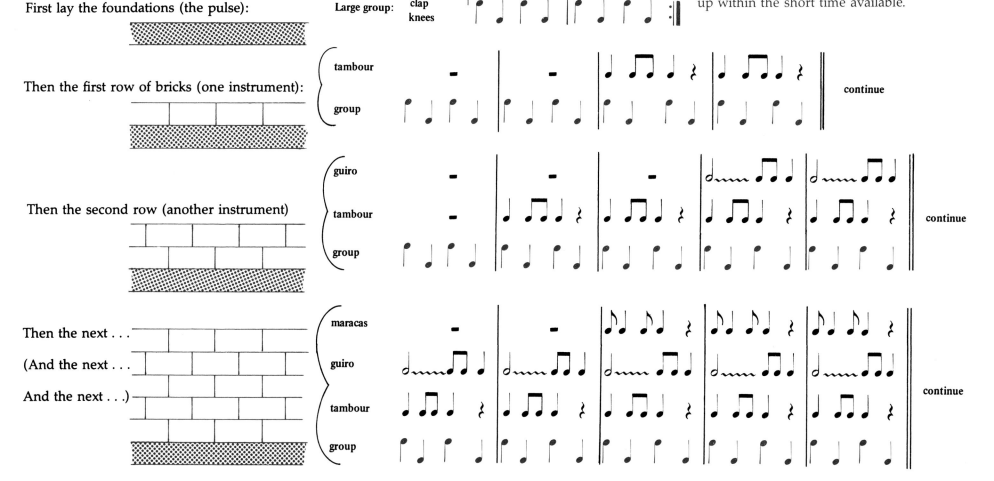

Fade-out...

> **Try** this activity during the musical interludes between Television programmes! (Instruments are not essential).

1 Give out an assortment of untuned instruments to as many, or as few of the class, as you wish

2 Play the chosen record.
The children listen. Each child, when ready to do so, either makes body percussion patterns, or instrumental patterns. Repeated patterns or improvisations are possible. *Quiet playing* is essential . . . ask each child to make sure he can *listen* to the record whilst playing. If he cannot hear it, he is too loud!

3 *Slowly turn down the volume* . . The children must continue to play, and should not get quieter with the music.
Listen to the texture formed . . . Try to keep together . . . Their patterns will begin to 'stand out' from the music, until, when the record is silent, only the instruments and body percussion sounds can be heard.

4 Slowly turn up the volume . . Have the children kept in time? If not, good listeners will quickly adjust by listening again to the record.

Street beat

Traditionally this was done in America by two parallel lines of boys on opposite pavements as they walked home from school. They usually accompanied it with "When the Saints go Marching in".

This is not as difficult as it looks. Start simply by repeating bar 1 several times. Each bar adds one extra sound and can be repeated as often as necessary. The final clap is done by hands imitating a cymbal clash.

keep those feet in time! Enjoy it!

At first, do it while marking time on the spot.

Try: Different formations in two lines.

What is it called?

You will need:

1. A selection of objects, or cards with large pictures
   e.g. shape recognition cards,
   coins,
   vase of flowers,
   leaves of well-known trees.
2. Four contrasting untuned instruments e.g. tambour,
   guiro, woodblock, indian bells.
3. Five tuned instruments, preferably different.

The Game:

● Choose one child to be the "Question-caller".

● Place by her one tuned instrument (e.g. bass xylophone) with two beaters.
● Place by her the set of objects or cards.
● She secretly chooses four of them and decides on an order.
● If she has a collection of pressed leaves, mounted on card, she might choose: Copper Beech, Horse Chestnut, Hawthorn, Oak.
● Allocate the four untuned instruments to four players. Place them in a row, numbered 1 to 4
● Allocate the remaining four tuned instruments to four players, numbering them 1 to 4.

Purpose:

1. To transfer word-patterns ⟹ clapping ⟹ untuned percussion ⟹ tuned percussion.
2. To improve memory and concentration

The following sequence should continue without a break. However, previous experience in transferring words patterns to instruments is essential (See pages 2–3). Some practice will be necessary, but the cards chosen should always be re–shuffled.

Q - "Question-caller"   C - Class

1 (Speech) Q holds up one card at a time	Q: "What is it called?" Q: "What is it called?"	C: "Copper Beech" C: "Hawthorn"	Q: "What is it called?" Q: "What is it called?"	C: "Horse Chestnut" C: "Oak"

NB: From now on the children must remember the names and order.

2 (Clapping)	Q: ♪♪♪	C: ♪♪	Q: ♪♪♪	C: ♪♪
	Q: ♪♪♪	C: ♪	Q: ♪♪♪	C: ♪

3 (Untuned instruments) Q quickly picks up two beaters and taps the question on the side of her xylophone. Untuned instruments answer in turn	Q: ♪♪♪	tambour ♪♪	Q: ♪♪♪	guiro ♪♪
	Q: ♪♪♪	woodblock ♪	Q: ♪♪♪	indian bells ♪

4 (Tuned instruments) Q plays the question on her xylophone. Tuned instruments answer in turn, using only 2 or 3 notes	Bass xylophone Q: 𝄞	Alto xylophone C: 𝄞	Bass xylophone Q: 𝄞	Alto glockenspiel C: 𝄞
	Bass xylophone Q: 𝄞	Soprano xylophone C: 𝄞	Bass xylophone Q: 𝄞	Soprano glockenspiel C: 𝄞

Ask the children to decide the ending: a coda could be added, maybe hearing the eight instrumentalists one by one, or responding to the cards shown in a different order.

A lucky dog

from *Nursery Nonsense* (Faber & Faber)

You will need: A rhyme appropriate to the disposition of your class. A selection of untuned instruments.

Purpose: To compose attractive accompaniments to a verse, using the device of ostinato building.

> *There was a young man of Bengal*
> *Who went to a fancy dress ball.*
> *He went just for fun,*
> *Dressed up as a bun,*
> *And a dog ate him up in the hall.*
>
> Anon

There are hundreds of suitable rhymes and verses that can be combined with an instrumental accompaniment.

Ask the children for suggestions for rhythmic patterns after familiarising them with the rhyme.

Some children will base their pattern on words in the rhyme, others will prefer to invent more freely.

Using their suggestions, build the accompaniment up gradually, one pattern at a time. Here is an example of a finished accompaniment.

Ostinato	Voices	Swanee Whistle	Guiro	Cymbal	Maracas	Two Tone block	Bongos

Score labels: Voices — "There was gal went ... ball, went up dog hall." "Woof" (Solo in own time)

32

Walk-about

You will need:

1. Up to six tambours
2. Varied selection of hand-held untuned instruments.
3. Instruments for the accompaniment or suitable record.
4. Optional: a recorder, if you feel confident enough to improvise.
5. Preferably room for a seated circle, but this activity can take place sitting at desks or tables.

1 Give out:
- six tambours
- untuned instruments to half of the class
- several tuned instruments. Include a guitar or cello if appropriate.
- or use a suitable record.

Accompanying group

2 Players on tuned instruments play ostinato patterns. Encourage bright rhythmical playing; the combined repeated patterns are to form the accompaniment, and need to be spirited.

3 Ask for suggestions to make a simple rhythm for the tambours. Decide on a pattern which can be easily memorised (if necessary use words to help).

These examples are in F pentatonic

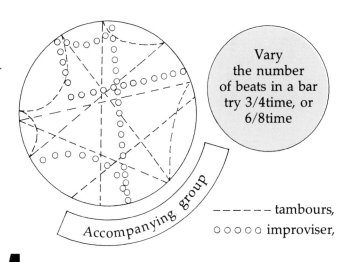

Vary the number of beats in a bar try 3/4 time, or 6/8 time

– – – – – tambours,
○ ○ ○ ○ ○ improviser,

Accompanying group

4 The accompanying group plays (and continues without stopping until the end).

The children with tambours lightly tap their remembered pattern. Each player, after several patterns, walks slowly over to any child **not already holding an instrument** taking an elaborate route if she wishes, playing all the time. She hands over the tambour.

Without a break the child who has received the tambour continues the pattern for a while before walking to someone else. The first player sits in her place. All six tambours are played simultaneously, but

each of the players will choose her own moment to move, so that they will not necessarily be walking around at the same time.

A recorder improvisation greatly adds to the spirit of this activity.

5 While the tambours continue to play their pattern (*very quietly*), one child is chosen who holds an untuned instrument (other than the tambours). The player improvises whilst walking over to any other child holding an untuned instrument. That child now begins own improvisation, she stands and walks over to another child. Meanwhile the first child stops playing and sits down in the second child's place.

Thus the following things will be happening simultaneously:

(a) Instrumental accompaniment (or record)
(b) six tambours, playing identical patterns, continuously changing hands
(c) An improvisation on another untuned instrument, continuously changing from player to player.
(d) Optional recorder improvisation

Ensure that the children are skilful in weaving around one another, so as to avoid collisions. Several children could well be walking around at the same time

6 Stop the activity when all the children have played at least once.

Purpose:

1. To give opportunity for improvising
2. To give a memorisation challenge
3. To give experience of playing while walking around.
4. To incorporate other instruments/records.

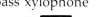

Bass xylophone

 or

with Alto xylophone   with Soprano xylophone

The players may alter their ostinato patterns from time to time.

*An extra note has been added here to F pentatonic.

Flea flied (Bounce those beaters!)

You will need: A selection of multitones
(see pages 25-7)

Essential previous experience:
Practice in transferring word patterns to instruments and later to instruments played with two beaters. (see page 7)

A simple accompaniment is necessary for all the following activities e.g.

$$\frac{4}{4}$$

on any two toned instrument, or... two sounds from one instrument. Strike a tambour with the felt beater head on the skin, followed by the handle on the rim, alternately.

One two three ★
Mother caught a flea ★
Flea flied, aunty died
One two three. ★

Purpose:
1. To transfer the rhythm of a whole rhyme to:
   (a) knees
   (b) multitones
2. To develop agility in using two beaters.
3. To gain experience of different phrase lengths.

Children will vary in developing dexterity and coordination. Physical tension may result from neglecting the above stages. It is quite normal for some children to be at stage 2 or 3 whilst others are tackling a complete multitone.

1 Chant the words rhythmically and with spirit. Each child claps at ★

2 Tap the rhythm of the words on *one* knee using both *hands, but not necessarily alternately,* whilst saying the rhyme. Tap the *other* knee likewise.

3 Tap the same rhythm on desk, floor or chair seat, using both hands in different R/L patterns.

4 Give out as many pairs of beaters as you have, ensuring that one is held in each hand. Tap the rhythm *gently* on desk, floor or chair, alternating beaters as above while the remaining children continue to practice with their hands. The beater movements must be light and bouncy. This develops facility without being restricted to exact locations on instruments.

5 Children who can manage this are ready to play the rhythm on *one* skull of the temple blocks or *one* part of any multitone. The remainder may either continue practising the rhythm, or clap at ★

6 Before using two tones (or two skulls) more knee practice is essential, using *both* knees.
Using the words of "Flea flied", give patterns for the children to copy e.g.

7 Transfer to *two* skulls or Temple Blocks, or multitones.

8 By now any child who can do this with ease will be ready to use three skulls, or parts of multitones without further preliminary work.

9 More tones can be used, if desired.

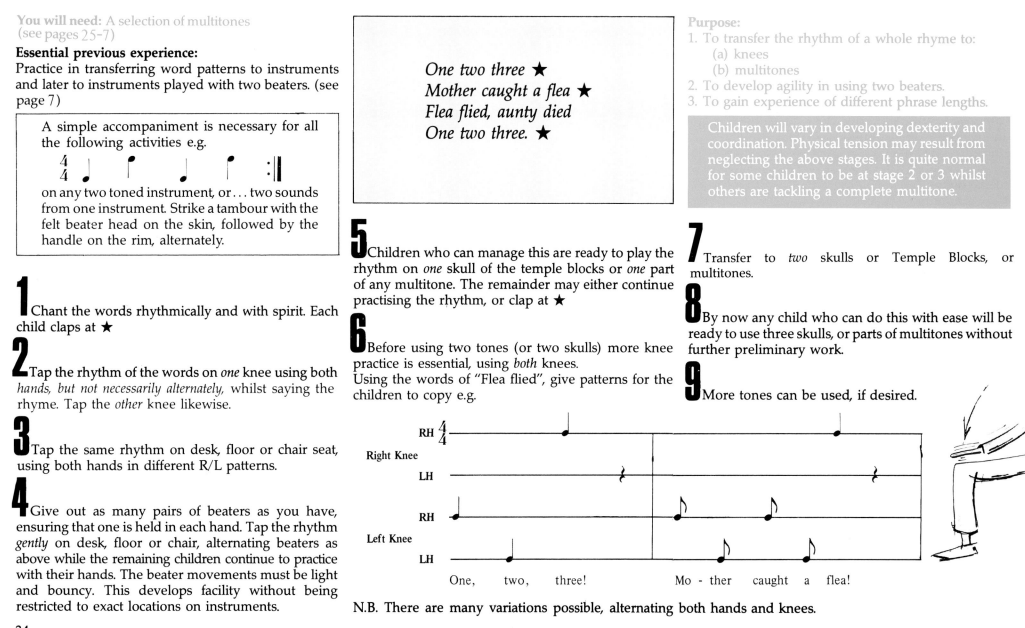

N.B. There are many variations possible, alternating both hands and knees.

Higglety, pigglety, pop! (fast beater bouncing)

You will need:
1. A collection of classroom percussion instruments.
2. A selection of "multitones" (see pages 25-7).

These rhymes have been chosen because their fast rhythms necessitate using two beaters. Choose a simpler rhyme, with the same *short–short–long* phrase pattern, if necessary.

The game

1 Children who have developed sufficient skill in using beaters with agility (see p.34) form two lines, meeting at the multitone. See ♦ in diagram. The first child in each line holds a pair of beaters. They will be playing the rhythmic pattern one after another.

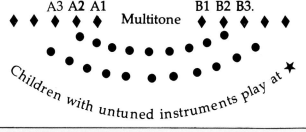

A3 A2 A1   B1 B2 B3.
Multitone

Children with untuned instruments play at ★

2 The remaining children sit around the multitone holding untuned instruments. See ● in diagram. At ★ they play a single, sharp short sound.

Higglety, Pigglety Pop! ★
The dog has eaten the mop; ★
The pig's in a hurry,
The cat's in a flurry,
Higglety, pigglety pop! ★

Keep the words *bright, lively* **and** *precise.*
Use tongues and lips!

---

(1)
Oh the Grand Old Duke of York★
He had ten thousand men★
He marched them up to the top of the hill and he marched them down again★
And when they were up they were up★
And when they were down they were down★
And when they were only half way up they were neither up nor down★

Purpose:
1. To develop agility in using two beaters.
2. To transfer the rhythm of a whole rhyme to instruments, or "multitones" (see p.25-7).
3. To gain experience of different phrase lengths.

3 The teacher plays a simple two-tone pattern such as:-

$$\frac{6}{8} \quad \text{♩. ♩. | ♩. ♩. :|}$$

4 The children in rows A and B take turns to play the rhythm of the words as follows:- A1 B1 A2 B2 A3 B3 etc. As soon as A1 has played he hands the beaters to the next in his row and walks to the end while B1 is playing. Thus A2 will be ready to follow B1. Each new player must begin immediately after the final ★ sound leaving no break in the rhythm.

---

(2)
I eat my peas with honey★
I've done it all my life★
It makes the peas taste funny
But it keeps them on the knife.★

(3)
Pethery Fethery Fell★
The Witches are making a spell★
They creep around without a sound
Pethery Fethery Fell★

Roundabout one

You will need:
1. The "special" instrument.
2. Accompanying multitone — Two tambours and one tambourine placed on floor with skins uppermost.
3. 'Roundabout' signal (cymbal)
4. Optional extra instrument(s) (maracas).
5. Space for a seated circle.

Preparation for Roundabout One and Two.

Seat children in circle.

Play a repeated pattern on the accompanying multitone while children make body percussion patterns. (Either a suggested pattern or an improvisation).

Explain that, when the accompaniment stops and the cymbal is trilled VERY QUIETLY (with the handle of one of the beaters) this is the roundabout signal which means STOP their patterns and SLIP SILENTLY into the next place. When they are settled, return to the original accompaniment and patterns. Player of accompaniment remains in the centre throughout.

● Practice this several times until the change is made smoothly.

Now Roundabout One can begin.

1 Place the special instrument in front of one child and maracas in front of another.

2 The children move around to the signals as before, each taking a turn at improvising on the special instrument.

● A child could take over the accompaniment.
● If numbers are large seat the children in two circles. Only the inside circle moves around. Next time, exchange places.

What is a Multitone? See pages 25-7

Purpose: To give a large number of children the chance to try out a special instrument (ie a new instrument, a multitone etc.)

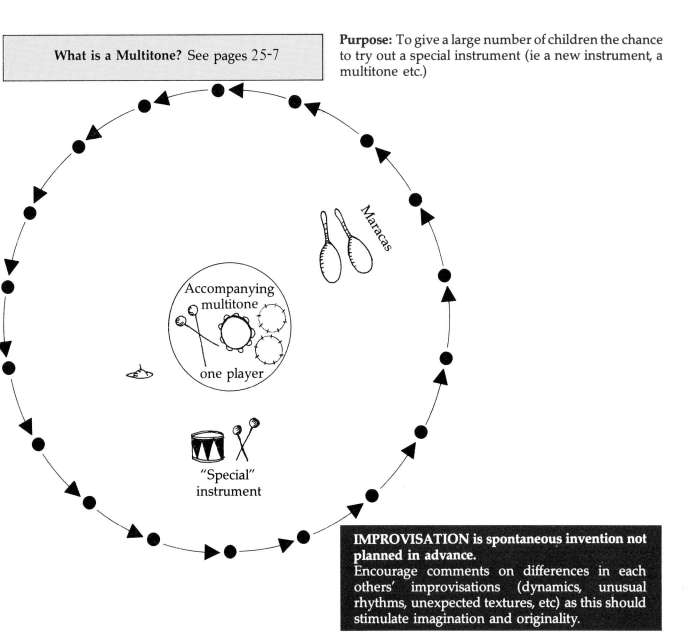

Maracas

Accompanying multitone

one player

"Special" instrument

IMPROVISATION is spontaneous invention not planned in advance.
Encourage comments on differences in each others' improvisations (dynamics, unusual rhythms, unexpected textures, etc) as this should stimulate imagination and originality.

Roundabout two

You will need:
1. Eight different untuned instruments.
2. Accompanying multitone (as in Roundabout One)
3. Space for two circles, one inside the other.

The players
- either play repeated patterns
- or improvise freely and explore the instruments. Meanwhile . . . the outer circle makes body percussion patterns, but **everyone** is silent at the tap of the cymbal.

Essential previous experience:
Practice in building one pattern on top of another, using untuned instruments (see page 29). The instruments must be played *quietly*.

Encourage:
- Correct technique
- Patterns suited to the instrument e.g. long sounds on a triangle.
- Listening to each other so that no one player drowns the rest!

Increase the challenge!

- Allocate a simple rhythm to one category of instrument e.g. metal or skin. When players reach these instruments they must remember to play this rhythm. Find a word/words to fit the rhythm if a reminder is needed.
- Place cards in front of some, and eventually all instruments. These can reinforce work in other areas. e.g. notation, word rhythms and variations of dynamics, timbre and duration.

This version works in the same way as Round-about One. The difference is that each child in the inner circle (not more than eight) will play an instrument at each change of place.

Purpose:
1. To give experience in a variety of untuned instruments.
2. To give further opportunities for exploring and improvising.

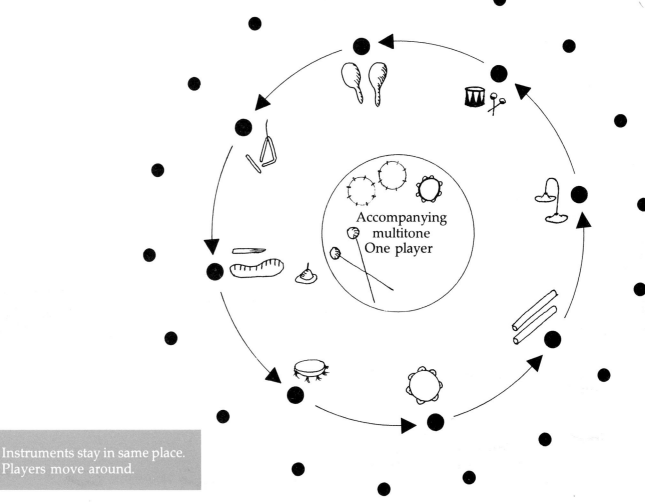

Accompanying multitone One player

Instruments stay in same place. Players move around.

Severe scolding (Make a rhythmic piece)

You will need: For **(C)** a selection of untuned instruments.

Beforehand:

1. Prepare a plausible but light-hearted story which will lead up to the scolding . . .

2. Discuss with the children the various dramatic qualities evoked by:
- quiet voices (or sounds) . . .
- loud voices . . .
- a gradual crescendo . . .
- a gradual diminuendo . . .

e.g. "Is quiet always gentle?"

   "Is loud always bright and happy?"

3. Discuss possible moods of the characters. e.g. "I really did try" could express various emotions, by means of inflection of voice, facial expression, intensity, and so on.

Suggested procedure:

1A
Children say **Red words (the adult role)**; the teacher says **Black words (the child role)**.

2
Exchange roles.

3
Add body percussion: **red words-clap; black words tap knees.**

4
Everyone takes both roles.

5
Try the body percussion rhythm without words. A simple accompaniment on bongos will help to keep the rhythm accurate.

6B
Two groups speak in canon, as in **(B)**.

7C
Group work:
Using a selection of untuned instruments, invent a piece which
- splits the rhythms between several instruments, whilst keeping strictly to the word rhythms and dynamics.
- retains the contrast between the two roles.

> Let your face and your voice show your **feelings!**

Purpose:
In **A** to express the contrasting moods, using dynamics, through speech and body percussion

In **B** to introduce canon

In **C** to transfer the speech rhythm to instruments, thus forming an independent piece.

The words of the conversation:

Adult (loudly):	**You've come late!**
Child (normal voice):	**I missed the bus and then the train . . .**
Loudly:	**You're always late!**
Quietly:	**I really did try . . .**
Crescendo- starting with a furious whisper:	**Everytime you visit me you're lazy and you're late for tea . . .**
Very loudly:	**You're always late!**
Quietly:	**I really did try . . .**

QUIET ⇨ soothing ⇨ peaceful ⇨ tired ⇨ ominous ⇨ stealthy ⇨ secretive ⇨ frightening ⇨ angry.

LOUD ⇨ exciting ⇨ powerful ⇨ angry ⇨ terrifying ⇨ aggressive ⇨ strong ⇨ happy ⇨ joyful.

A The rhythm of the words:

Red: clap
Black: tap knees

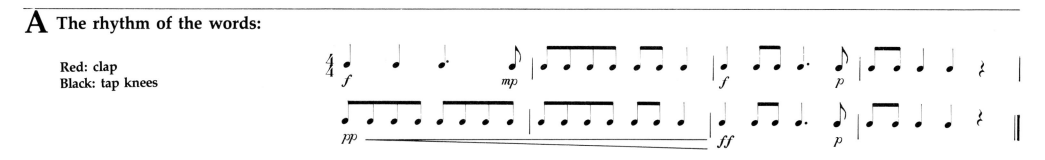

B For the canon . . . enter like this . . .

Group 1	You've come late! I	missed the bus and then the train . . .	You're always late! I	really did try . . . etc.
Group 2		You've come late! I	missed the bus and then the train . . .	You're always late! etc.

C From the words to the instruments:

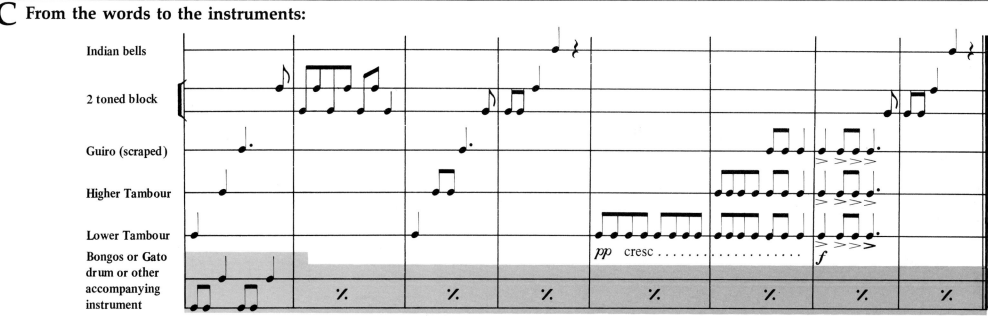

Indian bells
2 toned block
Guiro (scraped)
Higher Tambour
Lower Tambour
Bongos or Gato drum or other accompanying instrument

39

T.V. Tantrum
(from *Music for Children* Vol.I)

You will need Nothing for stages one and two. A selection of untuned instrument for stage three.

Remember to tap hands lightly when clapping fast.

Show that you feel *sulky, angry,* and other emotions by using your *voice and face expressively!*

Purpose:
1. To prepare for an instrumental piece using verse, and body percussion.
2. To relate dynamics to dramatic content.
3. To introduce two independent parts which link in only one place.

1

Stages 1 & 2
Before dividing the class into two groups try:
- Teacher as adult and class as child.
- Teacher as child and class as adult.

Adult	Turn the	T.V.	off and	go to	bed now.			
Child						Oh (sulkily)	no I	won't.
Adult (louder)	Turn the	T.V.	off and	go to	bed now.			
Child						Oh (angrily)	no I	won't
Adult (firmly)	Turn	it	off!		Go	to	bed.	
Child (crossly)	Ev-ery	time I	want to	watch a	prog-ramme	that I	real-ly	like, it's
Adult	If you	get no	sleep you	will turn	yellow			
Child	No					Oh	no I	won't!

3

Stage 3
The instrumental setting below is a suggestion. Let the children experiment and use their own ideas. Ideal for group work.

Timpani □ □ □ □ □ □ □ □ □ □						Guiro ✦ ✦ ✦ ✦~~~
Timpani □ □ □ □ □ □ □ □					Guiro ✦ ✦ ✦ ✦~~~	
Tambour 1 ○	Tambour 2 ○	Tambour 3 ◯		Tambour 1 ○	Tambour 2 ○	Tambour 3 ◯
Two-tone wood block ☆ ☆	☆ ☆	☆ ☆	☆ ☆	☆ ☆	☆ ☆	☆ ☆ ☆ ☆
□ □ □ □ □ □ □ □ □ □						
Two-tone wood block ☆					Guiro ✦ ✦ ✦ ✦~~~	

2

Adult clapping

Child clapping / stamping

Perplexity plus

(from *Music for Children* Vol. V)

You will need:
1 drum (low pitched)
1 wood block
1 set of multitones See p. 25-27
1 pair bongos and 1 cabasa
Optional: several other untuned instruments.

Divide the children into two groups facing each other. Group 1 will be trying to catch out group 2 which is quite determined not to be caught out!

First:
Teach the words as one continous part.
Then: Teacher takes Part 1, children take Part 2. (Make sure that the words are spoken very expressively and that voices rise at each question to contrast with the aggressive quality of the challenging group.)
Then: Change round so that children take Part 1.

The complete piece has three sections, following without a break:
Section 1. Speech (A)
Section 2. Speech with body percussion (B)
Section 3. Group 1 transfers body percussion rhythm to instruments; group 2 rises to the challenge of group 1 by performing the body percussion patterns (B) without words. Play A and B together.

Woodblock and drum accompany throughout the piece and are joined by bongos and cabasa in Section 3.

Purpose: To give experience in:-
1. Speech rhythms ⟶
   Body percussion ⟶
   Untuned percussion.
2. Cross rhythms
3. Antiphony

Group 1. Here is a rhythm to perplex you!
Group 2. Here is a rhythm to perplex us?
A Here is a rhythm to perplex you
    So let's try to catch you out!

This is how it ought to go. Oh yes?
This is how it ought to go. Oh yes!
B Just like this. Just like this?
    Just like this. This is how it ought to go!
    Oh yes? (disdainfully)

Section 1

Section 2

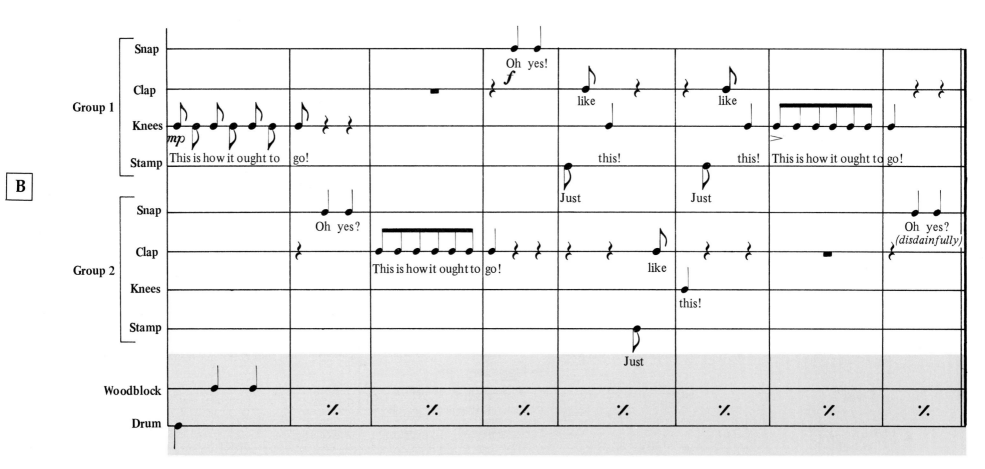

Section 3

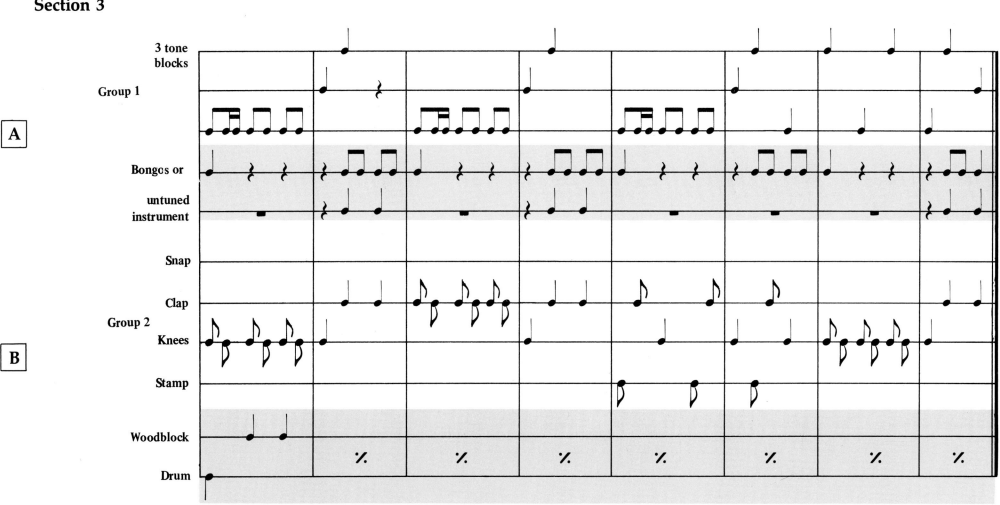